The Book of Silly Rhymes

Cheryl Lee-White

Illustrated by Louise Rarity

Published in the United Kingdom by:

Blue Falcon Publishing
The Mill, Pury Hill Business Park,
Alderton Road, Towcester
Northamptonshire
NN12 7LS
Email: books@bluefalconpublishing.co.uk
Web: www.bluefalconpublishing.co.uk

Copyright © Cheryl Lee-White, 2019

The moral right of the author has been asserted in accordance with the Copyright, Designs and Patents Act 1988.

All rights reserved. No part of this publication may be reproduced, stored or transmitted, in any form or by any means, without the prior permission in writing of the publishers.

This is a work of fiction. Names, characters, businesses, places, events and incidents are either the products of the author's imagination or used in a fictitious manner. Any resemblance to actual persons, living or dead, or actual events is purely coincidental.

A CIP record of this book is available from the British Library.

First printed 2019
ISBN 978-1912765126

To Bella, Lia, Alexa, Sophia
and my partner Dino,
thank you for all
the laughter you bring.

The Book of Silly Rhymes

Cheryl Lee-White

Mrs Balderdash

Our teacher Mrs Balderdash
has a great big moustache.
It is dark, black and hairy,
and it looks really scary!

School is Boring

School is so boring,
I am always snoring.
I want to be outside
playing on the hillside,
breathing in the fresh air
with the wind in my hair.

The Pencil Stealer

There's a girl in my class called Jo Feeler,
and she is a big pencil stealer!
Every lesson (without fail) she will ask
for a pencil to help do her task.
When we're finished, she won't give it back –
she hides it inside her backpack.

One day I had just had enough
of Jo Feeler the stealer of stuff.
The very best plan I could hatch
was to give my bum a good scratch
with the pencil she was going to use.
I don't think that she was amused!

Dodgeball

I don't like doing sports at school,
I don't like games; I don't like rules.
I think the very worst of all
must be the dreaded game – dodgeball.

I have a really awful aim,
so bad the ball hit Mr Benbain.
It smacked him hard right in the nose,
blood gushed and ran down to his toes.

He wasn't happy with me at all.
He made me run around the hall
until I couldn't carry on,
because I'd run a marathon!

The School Swimming Pool

The swimming lessons at my school
are carried out in our school pool.
The slimy steps
have all turned green,
it really needs a good old clean.

It's filled with plasters, leaves and flies,
the toxic water burns our eyes!
The rails all around are rusting,
it's really nasty and disgusting.

Tall Paul

There's a boy at my school called Paul, who's amazing at basketball.

No one can beat him
unless they are cheating,
because he is seven feet tall.

Queueing

While queueing up for lunch one day
a flying football came my way.
It bounced across the school courtyard
and then collided with me hard.
The big bump knocked me to the ground,
and everybody gathered round.
My skirt flew
right up in the air; the
whole school saw my underwear!

Nanna

Nanna's coming round for tea;
I really hope she won't kiss me.
She has black hairs all over her chin
and a big wart growing out of her skin.

Mum is Always Moaning

My mum is always moaning at me,
I wish she would just leave me be!

"Get ready for school!" I hear her call.

"Don't leave your rucksack in the hall!"

"Clean your shoes and brush your hair!
Tuck your shirt in! I despair!"

"Have you really cleaned your teeth?"
she gapes at me in disbelief.

"And don't leave dirty underwear
upon my lovely kitchen chairs!"

DIY Dad

My dad is useless at DIY,
although he really does give it a try.
Last week he tried to put up a shelf,
but it fell on his head and he hurt himself.

He once tried to fix our washing machine
but instead, he ended up causing a scene.
Water was pouring out everywhere,
so if Dad gets out his hammer – beware!

Jude the Stinky Little Dude

My little brother's name is Jude,
and he's a smelly little dude.
Don't be fooled – he may be dinky,
but that doesn't mean he isn't stinky!

His dirty nappies really whiff,
and none of us will take a sniff.

Crazy Mum

My mum is very crazy,
she is a nutty lady.
She likes to wear pyjamas
to ride on her pet llamas.

Grandma Never Says No

I'm moving in with my grandma,
'cause mum won't let me have a guitar.
Grandma would never tell me no –
she can't, because she loves me so.

I really,
really want
that guitar;
why can't
Mum
be like
Grandma?

Uncle Justin

My great Uncle Justin
is really very disgusting.
He has a jiggly jelly belly
and his feet are super smelly.

Sometimes, he uses his toes
to pick boogers out of his nose.

Messy Jesse

Our bedroom is always messy;
it's all down to my brother Jesse.
He always drops the clothes he wore
all around our bedroom floor.

His dirty pants are everywhere,
but Jesse really does not care.

Chocolate Spread

Me and my little brother Fred
are both obsessed with chocolate spread.
We eat it every day and night
and savour every single bite.
We spread it thickly on pancakes
and drizzle it on our cornflakes.
We love it on our morning toast,
but it tastes best on Sunday roast!

Grandad Todd

I love my Grandad Todd,
but he is a little odd!

On his head he has no hair,
and although he shouldn't care,
he puts on an Elvis wig
that is three sizes too big.

Stinky Fart

Oh dear, my belly is surely grumbling,
and my bottom has started rumbling.
I shouldn't have eaten that cherry tart –
I need to do a stinky fart
that smells like fish and rotten eggs!
I think we'll all need large nose pegs.

Mum's Had Too Much Wine

Christmas time, Christmas time, Mum's had too much wine.
She's dancing round the living room, waltzing with the kitchen broom.

Harry the Elf

I can't wait for the 1st of December
to see the return of a loved family member.
His name is Harry and he is our elf,
he loves to sit on our bookshelf.
He seems a cute and sweet little guy,

but there's a twinkle in this eye!

Every night when we are asleep,
all around the house he will creep.
He is always up to no good
like putting pants in my coat hood.
He once dyed all his hair bright pink
and went surfboarding in the sink!

He is a naughty little elf
who brings such trouble on himself,
but no matter what a mess he gets in,
he never fails to make me grin!
I'm counting down the days 'til he's here
to bring us fun and Christmas cheer.

It's Snowing

Snow, snow everywhere,
on the ground and in the air.
There is no school today;
we are heading out to play!

Having lots of
snowball fights
and sleighing
down from
dizzy
heights.

What I Want for Christmas

I've asked Santa for a giraffe.
Dad thinks I am having a laugh!
He said it'll never fit in his sleigh,
but I know Santa will find a way.

The Crazy Cat Lady

I live next door to a crazy cat lady,

her name is Mrs Shelia O'Grady.

She has around 500 cats

and all of them wear silly hats.

Her house is like a strange cat zoo,

filled with fifteen tonnes of poo.

Slime

Slime, slime, all gooey and gungy,
stretch it around just like a bungee.
Long and green like illuminous snot,
oh I love my slime a lot!

Brussels Sprouts

I truly hate Brussels sprouts.
Mum says they are good for me,
but I have my doubts.
They're round and slimy like layered green snot.
I really dislike them a lot.

Sweets

I love eating sweets,
they're the very best type of treat.
Whether they're hard, soft or sour,
I would still eat them every hour!

Brian the Lion

My favourite animal is a lion,
if I had one as a pet I'd call him Brian.
Mum says that I can't have one –
she thinks I'll end up in his tum!

Disgusting Dog Poo

I have just stepped in sticky dog poop,
it's all over my brand new boot!
The smell of it is terribly bad –
arrgghh! It makes me really mad.

A Boy Called Ned

There once was a boy called Ned,
who always wore pants on his head.
Wherever he'd go they would be on show,
and their colour was always bright red!

Mr Mcgrew

Poor Mr Peter Mcgrew
is a keeper at our local zoo.
He looks after the apes,
but can never escape
when the cheeky old things
throw their poo!

Nits

I have got nits in my hair,
and it really isn't fair.
I hope this special lotion works,
as they are driving me berserk!

My Fat Cat

I just saw a giant rat
running past my snoozy cat.
She just watched it run right by,
and it looked her in the eye!
She won't get up off her mat –
she's too lazy; she's too fat.

Funky Monkey

Funky Monkey was very chunky;
he snapped a tree (or maybe three).

He turned from chunky
into hunky –
now he's hunky funky monkey.

Chocolate Cake

I want to eat chocolate cake every day,
and it makes me really sad
that Mum said only on my birthday,
because chocolate cake is bad.

Toby Eats His Bogies

I have a friend called Toby,
who likes to eat his bogies.
He says that they taste nice,
like chewing on gooey rice.

Pizza

Pizza is my favourite dinner,
nothing beats it – it's my winner!
No other meal I eat comes close,
not even my mum's beef roast.

My favourite base is stuffed crust,
on my pizza it's a must.
That cheesy, oozing, melty base
is the most delicious taste.

Mrs McDitch Might Be a Witch

I wonder if old Mrs McDitch
could possibly be a real witch?
She has a wart at the end of her nose,
long spindly fingers and turned up toes.

When she laughs
it is more like a cackle,
she lives in a house
that is old and ramshackle.

Her cat is as black as it could be,
and she drinks weird-smelling tea.
I'm sure she sits at home making potions,
and using her broom to fly across the oceans.

I'm too scared to find out if it's true,
in case she turns me into a shrew!

Can you spot the differences in the two images below?

(There are six to find)

Can you work out which letters are needed to make the names?

H__r_ t_e __f

M_s Mc_i_c_

A B__ C_ll_d
N__

Can you help Jo Feeler, the pencil stealer, find her pencil?

Also by the author...

Pete the Cheeky Parakeet

When Pete the Parakeet's favourite person goes on holiday without him, he's left behind with the rest of the family – and they're not his biggest fans!

Will Pete realise that being the bird with the bad attitude won't get him anywhere?

This amusing rhyming tale will bring lots of laughter and learning to story time!

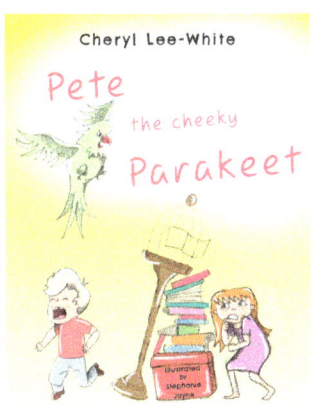

www.ingramcontent.com/pod-product-compliance
Lightning Source LLC
Chambersburg PA
CBHW042130100526
44587CB00026B/4249